Giselle's Songs of Praise

[1] indicates the song is from Giselle's CD *Heaven Is My Home*

[2] indicates the song is from Giselle's CD *I Believe In Jesus*

A Hiding Place

Based on Psalm 32:7

Words and Music by Giselle Tkachuk

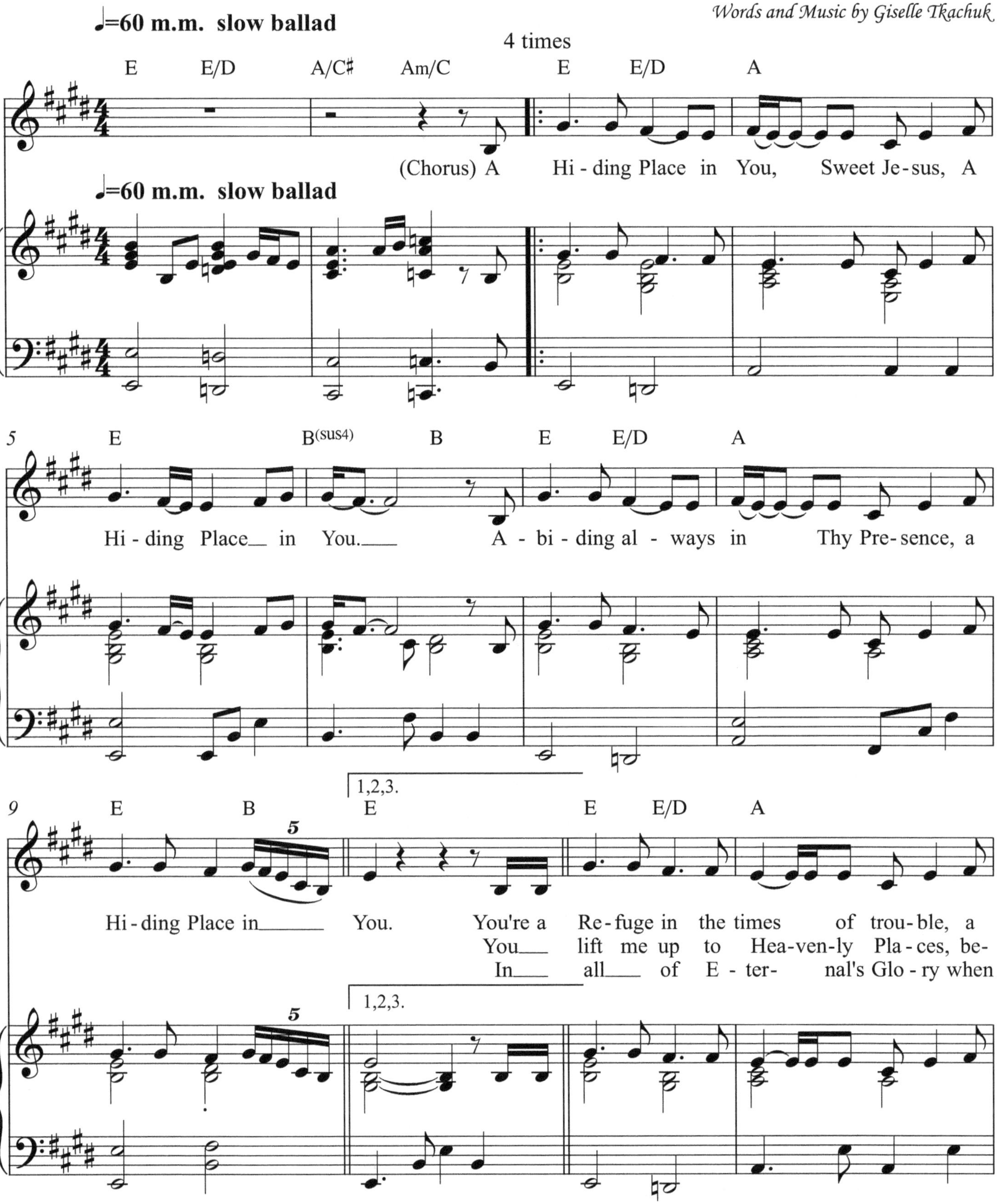
♩=60 m.m. slow ballad
4 times
E E/D A/C♯ Am/C E E/D A
(Chorus) A Hi - ding Place in You, Sweet Je - sus, A
♩=60 m.m. slow ballad
5
E B(sus4) B E E/D A
Hi - ding Place in You. A - bi - ding al - ways in Thy Pre - sence, a
9
1,2,3.
E B E E E/D A
5
Hi - ding Place in You. You're a Re - fuge in the times of trou - ble, a
You lift me up to Hea - ven - ly Pla - ces, be -
In all of E - ter - nal's Glo - ry when
1,2,3.
5

13

E   B(sus4)   B   E   E/D   A

Shel - ter from the storm,___ a Shield of safe - ty in the bat - tle, sur
side Your Glo - ri - ous Throne._ Con - tent to kneel be - fore Thy foot - stool__
I be - hold__ Your Face,_____ sat - is - fied with Thy Like -ness, for

17

E   B   E   B(sus4)   B   E   E/D

4.

roun - ding me___with songs. A you___ A - bi - ding al - ways
claim-ing this Place my ver-y own.
e - ver my Hi - ding Place.
B

4.

A   E   B   E   E/D   A/C♯   Am/C   E

a tempo

in Thy Pre - sence, a Hi - ding Place in_____ You

rit.

a tempo

rit.

All The Days Of My Life

Based on Psalm 27:4

Words and Music by Giselle Tkachuk

♩ = 110 m.m. rock ballad (half-time feel)

One thing I've asked that I shall seek from the Lord, that I may dwell in the House of the Lord. One thing I've asked that I shall seek from the Lord,

Lyrics:

that I may dwell in the House of the Lord. All the days

of my life, all the days of my life.

To be - hold the beau - ty of the Lord, all the days

5

of my life, and to me - di - tate in His Tem - ple,

all the days____ of my life

1.

2.

Yes, to praise_____ Your Most Ho - ly Name____ all the

days_____ of my life. Yes, to Praise_____ Your Most

Ho - ly Name,_____ all the days_____ of my

life

As for Me

Based on Psalm 73:28

Words and Music by Giselle Tkachuk

Lyrics:

(Chorus) As for me, the near-ness of God is my good._____ As for me, the near-ness of God__ is my good. On-ly He_____ can calm my trou-bled seas._____ As for me the near-ness of God is my good.

1.When Je - sus comes in-
2.Thy right Hand

to the place where I stand, the stor-my winds are hushed at His com
has ta - ken hold of me and I am al - ways safe - ly by Your

mand. His words to me: Peace, be still it is
side. You will guide, and lead me on to

I,_____ we're on our way_____ to the Oth-er Side. As for good. As for

Glo - ry, where in Your Pre-sence for-e-ver I'll a - bide.

me,_____ the near-ness of God_ is my good.

Dedication Song

Based on Mark 9:37

Words and Music by Giselle Tkachuk

Lyrics:

Verse lines (mm. 5–8):

lit - tle child,_ a pre-cious child, has been gi - ven in - to our care, and

child of God_ may you be blessed_ to know the Lord__ all your days, to

Ho - ly Word_ be un - to you__ a Lamp and Light un - to your feet, to

Verse lines (mm. 9–12):

on this day__ we de - di - cate this ten-der life un - to the Lord.

sing His praise,__ be wit-ness of his ten-der mer - cies and His love.

al-ways walk__ the nar-row way 'till safe-ly through the Pear-ly gates.

11

13 Chorus

And we praise our Heav'n-ly Fa - ther for His gra-cious lo-ving-kind - ness

17

to have shown us such com - pas - sion in the sha-ring of this life.

21

We'll en-dea-vour to be mind - ful that this soul is on a jour - ney.

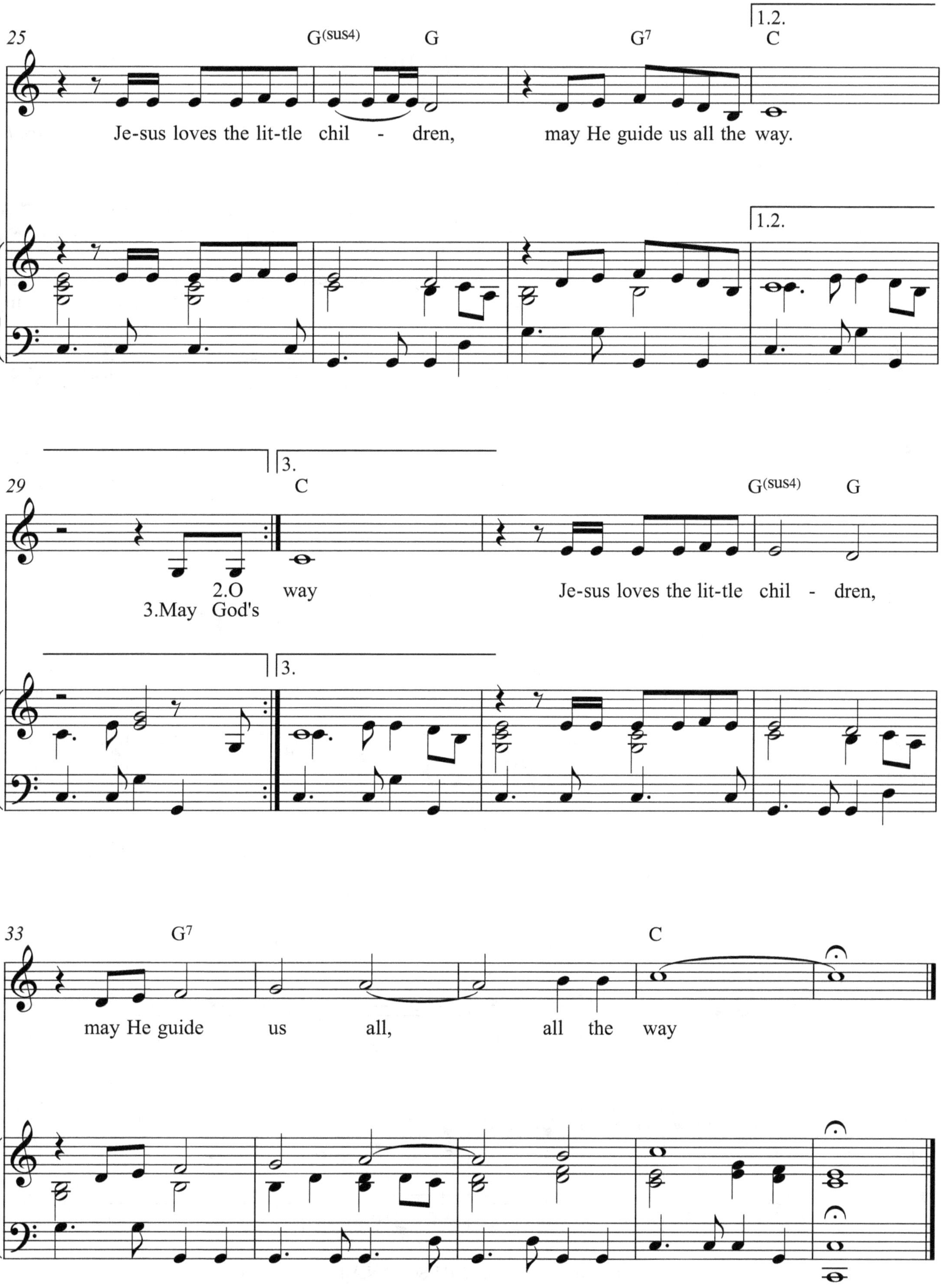

25
G(sus4) G G7 1.2. C
Je-sus loves the lit-tle chil - dren, may He guide us all the way.
1.2.
29
3. C G(sus4) G
2.O way Je-sus loves the lit-tle chil - dren,
3.May God's
3.
33
G7 C
may He guide us all, all the way

For God Only

Based on Psalm 62:1,5

Words and Music by Giselle Tkachuk

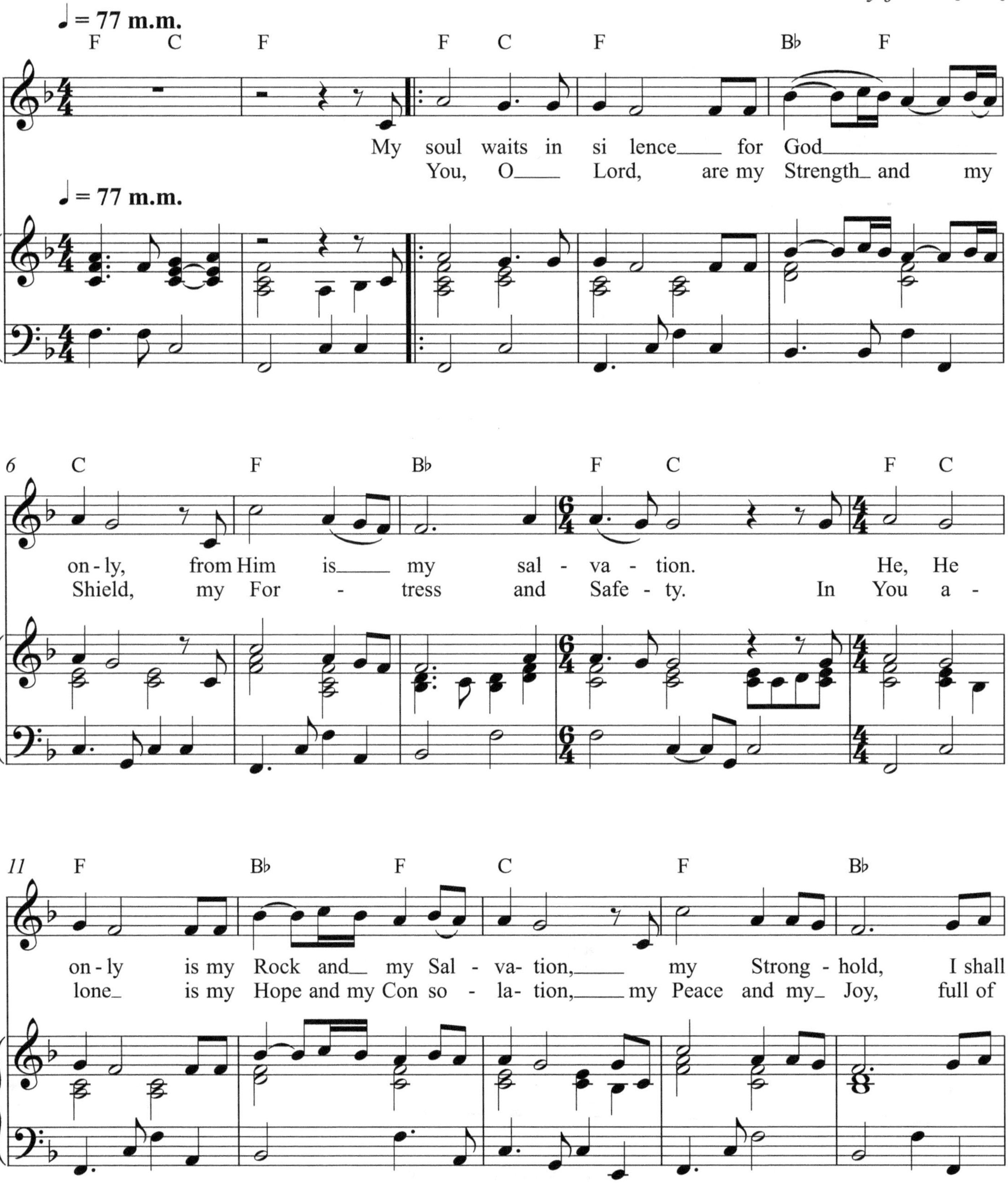

♩ = 77 m.m.
F C F F C F B♭ F
My soul waits in si lence for God
You, O Lord, are my Strength and my
♩ = 77 m.m.
6 C F B♭ F C F C
on - ly, from Him is my sal - va - tion. He, He
Shield, my For - tress and Safe - ty. In You a -
11 F B♭ F C F B♭
on - ly is my Rock and my Sal - va- tion, my Strong - hold, I shall
lone is my Hope and my Con so - la- tion, my Peace and my Joy, full of

not__ be great - ly__ sha - ken, I shall not be great-ly__ sha - ken.

Glo - ry. My soul waits in si - lence, for

God_____ on - ly. From Him is____ my Sal - va - tion.

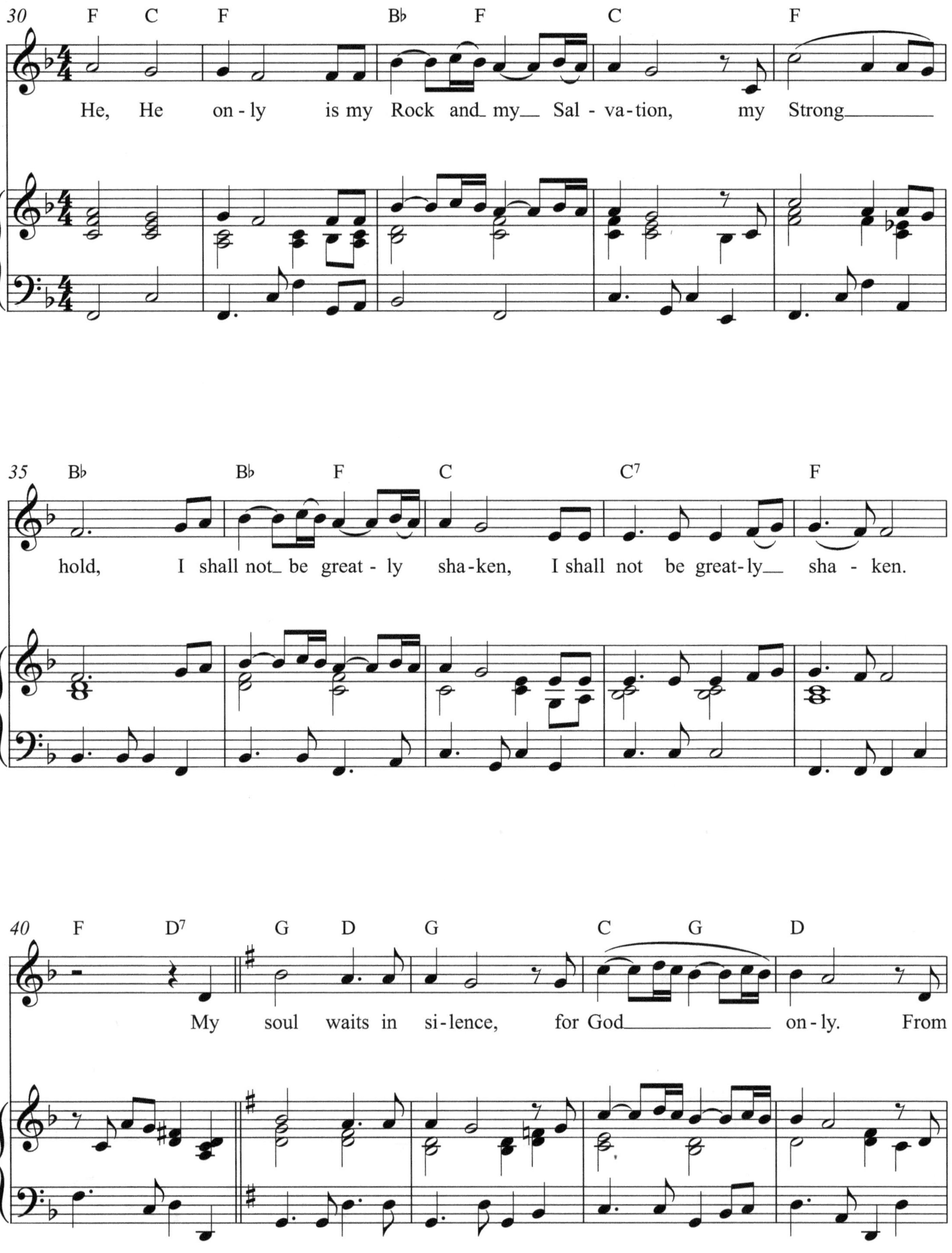

30
F C F Bb F C F
He, He on - ly is my Rock and my Sal - va - tion, my Strong
35
Bb Bb F C C7 F
hold, I shall not be great - ly sha - ken, I shall not be great - ly sha - ken.
40
F D7 G D G C G D
My soul waits in si - lence, for God on - ly. From

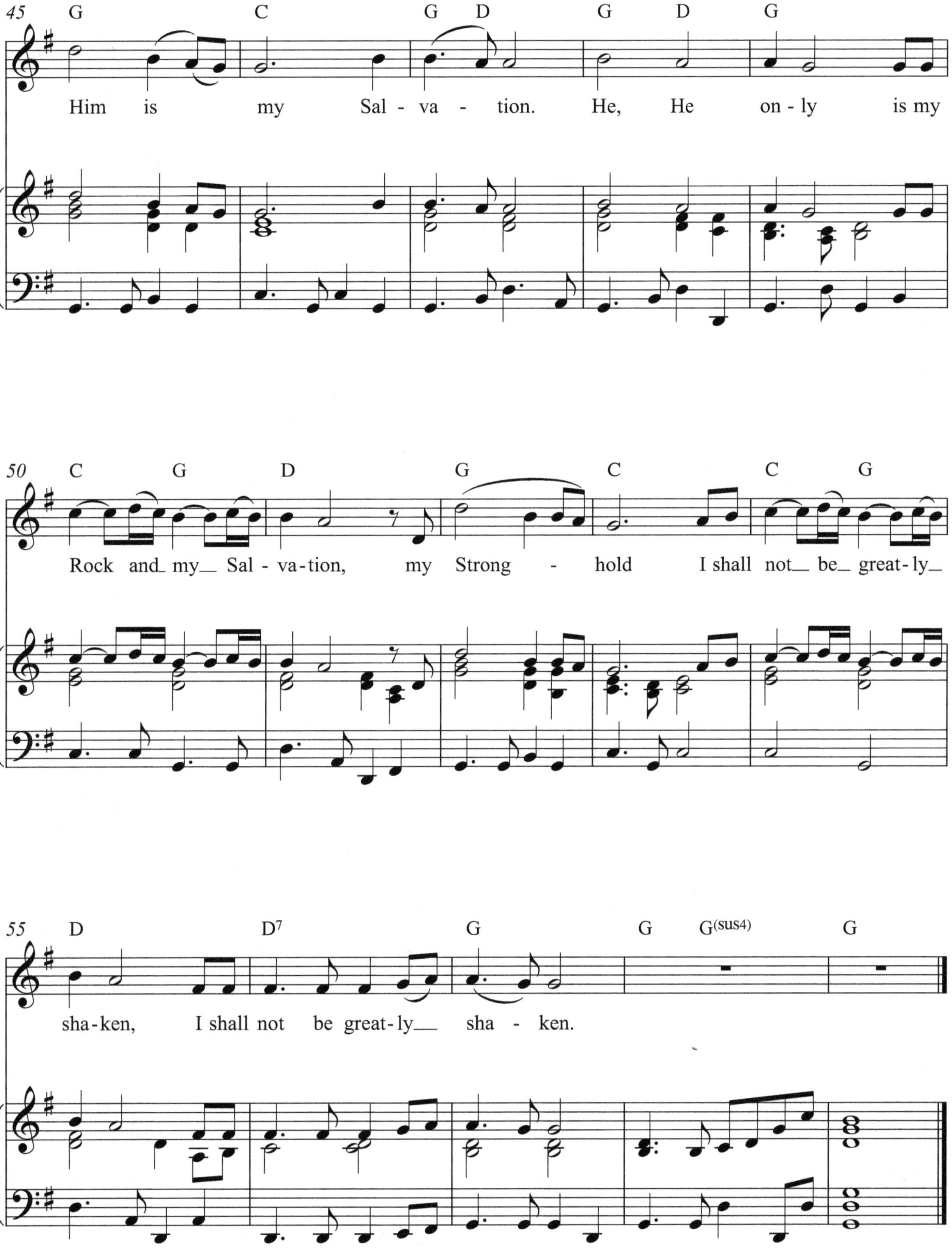

45
G C G D G D G
Him is my Sal - va - tion. He, He on - ly is my
50
C G D G C C G
Rock and_ my_ Sal - va - tion, my Strong - hold I shall not_ be_ great - ly_
55
D D7 G G G(sus4) G
sha - ken, I shall not be great - ly_ sha - ken.

Fountains of Blessings

Based on Revelations 22:1

Words and Music by Giselle Tkachuk

1.Foun - tains of
2.Ri - vers of
3.O - ceans of
4.Streams of a -
5.Ra - di - ance of

bles - sings, flo-wing from the Mount of God. Foun - tains of bles - sings
ho - li - ness, flo-wing from the Throne of God. Ri - vers of ho - li-ness
right-eous-ness pour-ing from the Son of God. O - ceans of right-eous -ness
noin - ting, flo-wing from the Courts of God. Streams of a - noint - ting
Glo - ry, glo-wing from the Face of God. Ra - di-ance of Glo - ry

11

flo-wing from the Mount of God. Flo - wing, flo - wing,
flo-wing from the Throne of God Flo - wing, flo - wing
pour-ing from the Son of God Pour - ing, pour - ing
flo-wing from the Courts of God Flo - wing, flo - wing
Glo-wing from the Face of God Glo - wing, glo - wing,

15

flo-wing from the Mount of God. Foun - tains of bles - sings,
flo-wing from the Throne of God. Ri - vers of ho - li - ness,
pour-ing from the Son of God. O - ceans of right - eous - ness,
flo-wing from the Courts of God. Streams of a - noin - ting,
glo-wing from the Face of God. Ra - di ance of Glo - ry,

19

flo-wing from the Mount of God.
flo-wing from the Throne of God.
pour-ing from the Son of God.
flo-wing from the Courts of God.
glo-wing from the Face of God.

1,2,3,4   5.

God.

1,2,3,4   5.

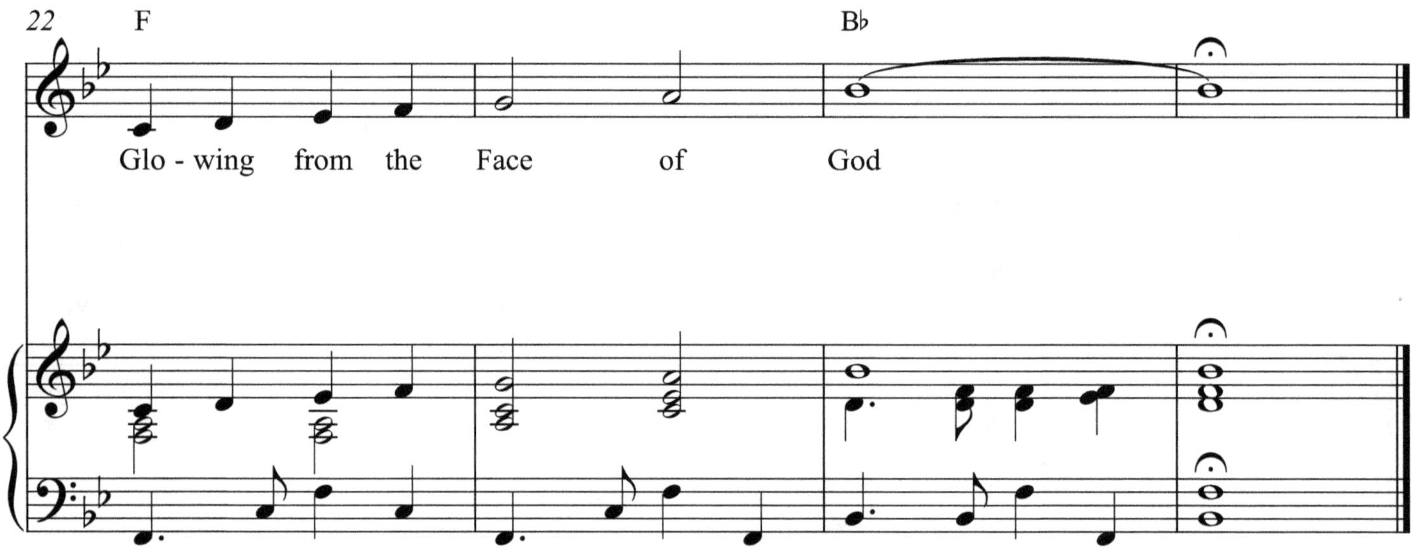
22
F
B♭
Glo - wing from the Face of God

Greater Than All

Based on Psalm 47

Words and Music by Giselle Tkachuk

Lord Most High is to be feared, a Great King o-ver all the earth.

prai - ses to our God, sing prai - ses, sing prai - ses to our King, sing prai - ses, for

He sub dues_ the na - tions un - der His Peo - ple. He

God a - lone_ is King____ o - ver all the earth.____ God

13 Em Am

choo-ses our in-he - ri-tance, Ja-cob's Glo - ry whom He loves, He as-
reigns o-ver all the na - tions, He sits up-on His Ho - ly Throne, the

17 Em B

cen-ded with a shout A trum-pet sound. And in this
Shields of the earth be-long to Him a - lone.

22 Em Am Em

mo - ment, I'll sing His prai - ses, For He is Grea - ter than
(last time) I'll praise You, Je - sus, for You are Grea- ter than

Lyrics:

27
all, and great-ly to be feared! I'll clap my hands, I'll shout for

32
joy, for He is so much grea-ter than all,___ and great - ly
(last time) For You are so much grea-ter than all,___ and great - ly

36
to be praised.___
to be praised.___

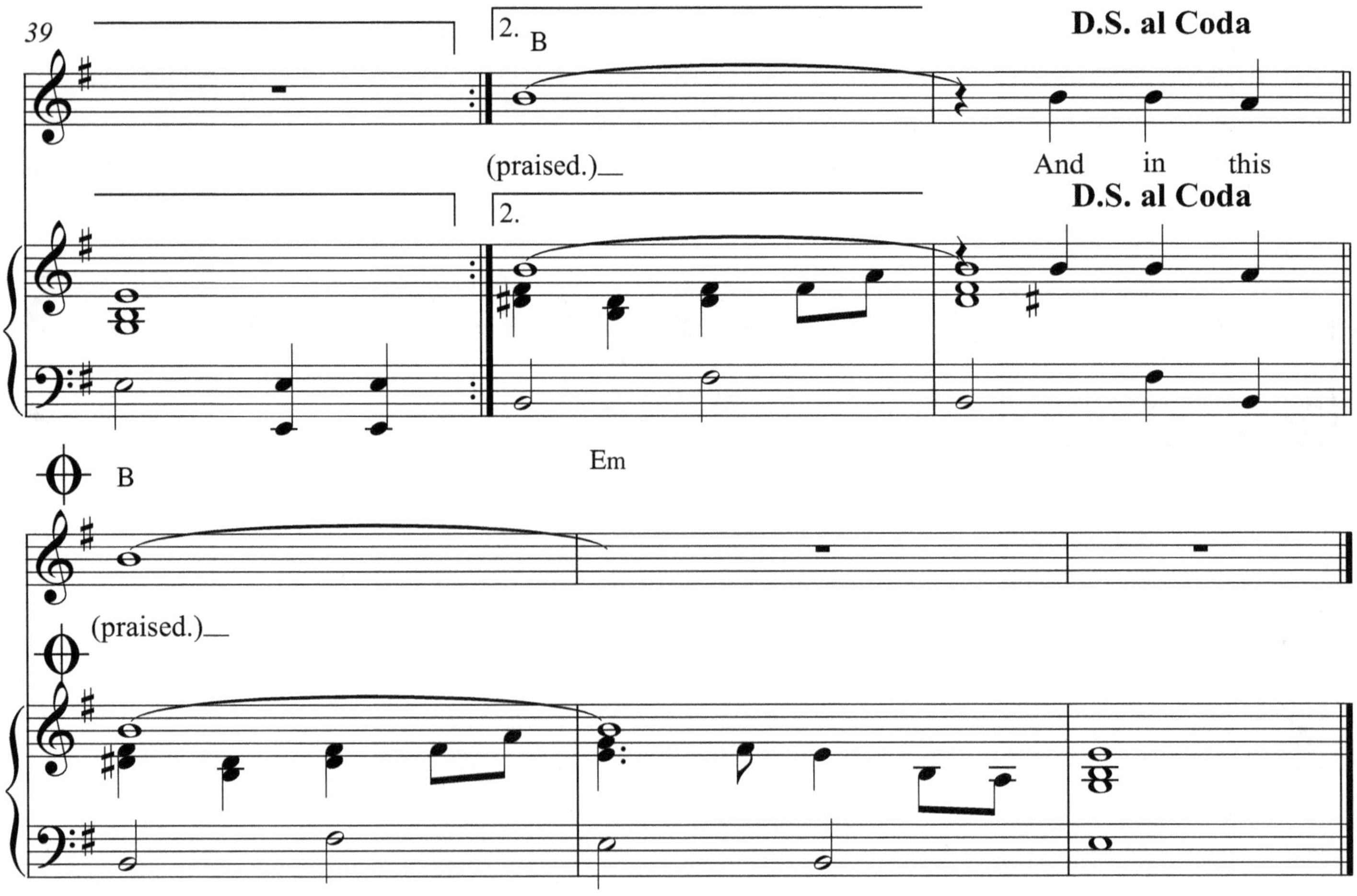
39
2.
B
D.S. al Coda
(praised.)
And in this
D.S. al Coda
2.
Em
B
(praised.)

Heaven Is My home

Based on John 14:3

Words and Music by Giselle Tkachuk

(Chorus) Well, no mat - ter how beau-ti-ful all this has been,___ I know that I'm_ on-ly pas - sing through._ And no mat - ter how beau - ti - ful___

15 G   D   A   **To Coda**

all this could e - ver be,___ I know___ that Hea-ven is my___

To Coda

19 1.2.   D   D(sus4)   D   D   G

Home.   1.Je - sus said: "I___ go to pre - pare a___
          2.All this earth - ly gla - mour and this earth-ly___

24   D   A   A(sus4)

place for you,___ that where I___ am_____ you may be al - so."
glor - ry___ could ne - ver_____ com - pare with my Lord._____

28
A
D
G
Je - sus said: "I am the Way, I am the
Just one mo - ment in His Pre - sence fills all my
32
D
A
D
Truth, the Life" and soon He'll be back to take me home.
long - ing needs, and soon I'll be with Him for - e - ver - more.
36
D
A6
3.
D
D(sus4) D
D
A
(Chorus) Well no Home. Do you know that Hea-ven Is your
3.

Home? (Chorus) Well, no Home. I

D.S. al Coda

know___ that Hea-ven Is My_ Home.

I Am Waiting For The Lord

Based on 2 Timothy 4:8

Words and Music by Giselle Tkachuk

Lyrics:

I am wait - ing, for the Lord, to ap - pear in the Eas - tern Sky, where He'll beck - on me to come, and re - ceive me to His side.

"As sure - ly as I live", You said,   Your
No more tears nor cry - ing There,
Your Good-ness o - ver-whelms me, Lord,   Your

Glo - ry would fill all the earth,   and though I've known Your Bless - ed-
no more fears, nor dy - ing There,   Your Pre - sence and your smile, O
Great - ness_ e - ven more,   but to see the joy up - on Your

ness,   my be - ing longs to see Your Face.
Lord,   and Your wel - come, more than my re - wards.
Face,   when You lead me through the pear - ly Gates.

I am I am wait - ing_____ for the Lord.
(2)You,

On that day,_____ He'll be cal - ling me cal-ling
(2)You'll

me to His ve - ry Pre - sence where I'll live_____
(2)Your

47
D
1.
2.
D
A
e - ter - nal - ly
I am
Where I'll
live
52
D
e - ter - - nal - ly
55
G/B
A/C♯
D

I Will Bow

Based on Psalm 17:15

Words and Music by Giselle Tkachuk

Lyrics:

I Will Bow be-fore Your Throne of Glo- ry, on the day_____ when I a-wake.

I will cast my-self__ be-fore Your Throne of grace, the ve-ry mom-ent I see you Face to face, the ve-ry mo-ment I see You Face to face.

Un-til then, with-in my heart, I bow down,

I bow down. Un-til then, with all my heart,

Lyrics:

I bow down, sweet Jes-us I bow down. I bow down be- fore Your Ma - jes - ty, I bow down be- fore Your Right - eous - ness, I bow down be- fore Your Ho - li - ness, I bow down,

I bow down, I bow down, sweet Jes-us I bow down.

For to see You in all your glor'-ious splen -
I will Bow be-fore Your Throne of Glo -

dor, is far more than my eyes could ev - er take. And for
ry, on the day when I a-wake. I will

all   Your man - - i - fold good - - ness   You've be-stowed___ on
cast   my self____ be-fore Your Throne   of grace,   the ve - ry mom - ent   I

such low - ly   es - tate,   You've be   stowed_   on my low - ly   es - tate.
see You Face to face,   The ve - ry mom - ent   I   see   You Face to face.

I bow   Face to   face,_____

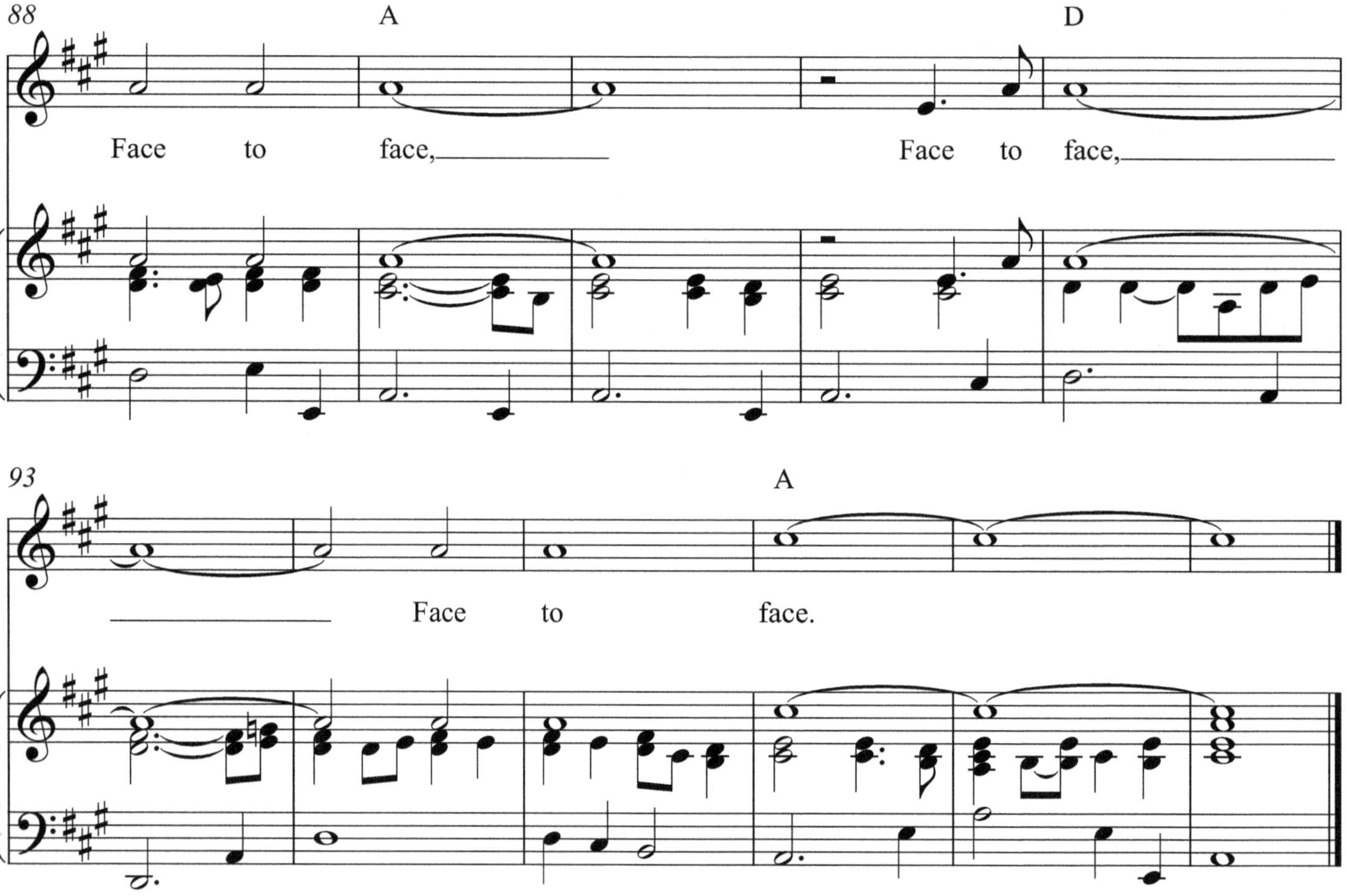
88
A
D
Face to face,
Face to face,
93
A
Face to face.

I'm Just A Pilgrim

Based on Matthew 25:21

Words and Music by *Giselle Tkachuk*

Lyrics:

1.I'm just a pilgrim
2.Though the road be
(3.I'm) bound___ for the

on a jour - ney to the land of my joy.
long that I must tra - vel, and some-times hard___ may be the wait.
New___ Je - ru - sa - lem___ to the Home___ of my joy.

My soul is long ing___ for the King - dom pro-mised me___
He that hath pro - mised is faith - ful, and will sure - ly
There___ the true___ and faith ful ser - vants will en - ter to___

by my Lord. He's gone be - fore me to make it re - ady,
not de - lay. Though I see dim - ly, and should He tar - ry
meet their Lord. He'll bid them wel - come, lay down your bur - dens,

and said some day that He'd re - turn. He's gone be - fore me
some day I'll see Him Face to face. Though I see dim - ly,
en - ter in your Fa - ther's joy, He'll bid us wel - come,

to make it re - ady, and said some day_____ "I
He will not tar - ry, so soon I'll see Him_____ Your
the jour-ney's en - ded, en - ter in_____

40

Lyrics (vocal line):

36 — shall re - turn." / Face to face / Fa - ther's Joy.
His Name is Je - sus,

42 — His Name is Je - sus, Mes-si-ah King, Lord of Lords.

48 — His Name is Je - sus, His Name is Je - sus, Mes-si-ah

53 A **To Coda** Dm

King, and Lord of Lords.

To Coda

59 **3rd time D.S. al Coda**

3.I'm

3rd time D.S. al Coda

Dm

Lords.

The Great I Am

Based on Exodus 3:14

Words and Music by Giselle Tkachuk

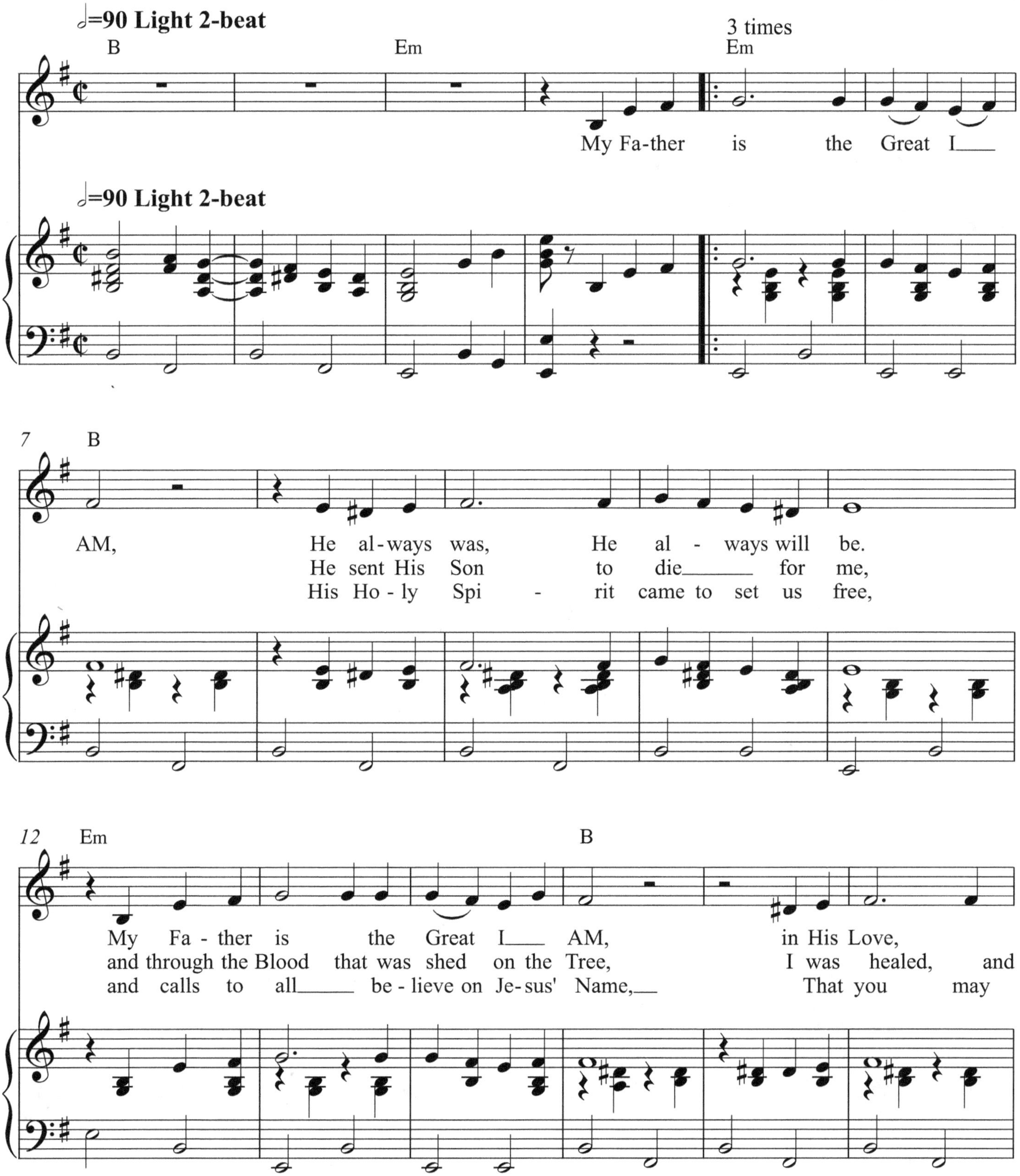

Lyrics (melody line):

My Fa-ther is the Great I___ AM,

He al-ways was, He al-ways will be.
He sent His Son to die_____ for me,
His Ho-ly Spi - rit came to set us free,

My Fa - ther is the Great I___ AM, in His Love,
and through the Blood that was shed on the Tree, I was healed, and
and calls to all_____ be - lieve on Je-sus' Name,___ That you may

He has set me free!
now I am free!
be__ set__ free!

O The Great I AM, the Great I

AM, He al - ways was,_ He_ al ways will be. The Great I
He sent His Son_____ to die__ for me, and through the
His Ho - ly Spi-rit came to set__ us free, and calls to

AM,_____ the Great_____ I AM, in His Love, He has set_____ me
Blood that was shed on the Tree, I was healed,__ and now_ I'm
all be lieve on Je-sus' Name, that you may_____ be__ set__

36 Em
1.2.
3.
Em Am
free! free! free!
2,3.My Fath-er
And calls to
42 Em B
all be - lieve on Je - sus' Name, that you may
47 B7 Em
be set free!

There Is a Home There for Me

Based on John 14:3

Words and Music by Giselle Tkachuk

1,6.There   is   a   Home there for me,

2.(My)   Sa - viour Je - sus will be   there,

3.(With) pre - cious Stones are built the   walls,

4.(He)   shed   His Blood on Cal - v'ry's Tree,

5.(And)   soon He'll be back to take me Home,

there   is   a   Home_____ there for__   me._____
He's   built   a   Home for me__ O   so fair._____
there's   room for one, there's room   for__ all._____
that   bought   a   Home there for you and__ me._____
where I'll praise His Name for - e - ver__ more._____

E⁷   A   A⁷   D

Far   be - yond   the   Jor - dan, with streets of Gold and a Cry- stal_ Sea, there

A   E   A   1-5   6.

is_____   a   Home__ there__ for me

2.My   There
3.With
4.He
5.And
Repeat verse 1 6.There

1-5   6.

47

is_____ a Home_____ there_____ for me

Therefore Shall I Boast In My Weakness

Based on 2 Corinthians 12:9

Words and Music by Giselle Tkachuk

Lyrics (voice line):

There - fore shall I boast in my weak-ness O Lord, that Your po-wer may rest up-on me._____ There-fore shall I boast in my weak-ness, O Lord, that your po-wer, O

Lord, may rest up - on me. I prayed as Your

ser - vant Paul re - move this thing from me, it's too hard for me to

bear. In Your Wis - dom You spoke, "My grace is suffi- cient for thee,___ for when you are weak___ my child, then

I___ am___ strong." There - on me There -

fore shall I boast in my weak - ness, O Lord___ That your po-wer may rest up - on me._____ There - fore shall I boast in my

weak - ness, O Lord__ That your po - wer__ O Lord may

rest, may rest, may rest up- on__ me_____

You Abide, O Lord

Based on Psalm 22:3

Words and Music by Giselle Tkachuk

Lyrics (vocal line):

You A - bide, O Lord,__ in the prai - ses_____ of Your peo__ ple, You A - bide._____ You A - bide, O Lord,_____ in the prai - ses_____ of Your

19 G — D — A — D — A

peo - ple, come, a - bide_____ in my praise,_____ come a-

25 D — G — A — D

[1,2]

bide. Come and dwell____ with - in____ my praise,
Lord I praise You with all of my heart,

30 G — A — D — G

come and live____ with - in____ my heart, come and make__ Your
Lord I praise You with all of my might, Lord I praise You with

36
A D G G A
Pre - sence known to me, a - bide with - in my
my en - ti - re be - ing, all Glo - ry to Your
42
D D D
life. You A - bide. Come a - bide
Name.
3
3
A D A D G D
in my praise, come a - bide.

www.ingramcontent.com/pod-product-compliance
Lightning Source LLC
Chambersburg PA
CBHW062109090426
42741CB00015B/3369